D0915079

BREW

A GRAPHIC GUIDE TO HOME BREWING

BREW

A GRAPHIC GUIDE TO HOME BREWING

AMMONITE PRESS

Mitch Adams

foreword by Mark Tranter

For Sarah – an extremely understanding beer widow,
more than ever whilst writing this book.

First published 2017 by
Ammonite Press
an imprint of Guild of Master Craftsman Publications Ltd
Castle Place, 166 High Street, Lewes, East Sussex, BN7 1XU,
United Kingdom

Text © Mitchel Adams, 2017
Copyright in the Work © GMC Publications Ltd, 2017

ISBN 978 1 78145 278 3

A catalogue record for this book is available from the British Library.

Publisher: Jason Hook
Designer: Robin Shields
Editor: Jamie Pumfrey
Consultant Editor: Mark Tranter
Illustrator: Rob Brandt

Colour reproduction by GMC Reprographics
Printed and bound in China

CONTENTS

FOREWORD

Beer is the most sociable of drinks. It inspires us, divides us and compounds us. The salutation between friends, the clink of glass, the first sip and the satisfied soul.

As beer becomes ever more popular and information more and more widely available, so does peoples' thirst grow – both for beer itself and for the history and science behind it. The lust for knowledge that our species exhibits, usually manifests itself in practical application.

Homebrewing was, not so long ago, more of a hangover from the 1970's – awful parsnip wine and flat brown bitter – a way of saving money whilst meting out punishment on your friends and family. Even in the mid-1990's when I started homebrewing, John Bull bitter kits, were *de rigueur*, whilst food bags with some crushed barley and last year's goldings hops, drying further in the shop window, were positively exotic. Information was limited to a few publications, so – with a little help – you taught yourself.

Now, information is immediate. Ingredients are of commercial quality. Beer styles from many countries are known and understood. This book you hold, is an excellent and fun way to get into brewing, an in-depth overview to get you well on your way to producing your own beer. Good Beer! Making good beer is as easy as making bad beer – it just takes some understanding. So use the resources available to you but find your own way too, when you make mistakes, learn from them and understand what went wrong – mistakes teach us so much. Stouts, Porters, Pale Ales, Lagers, Saisons, Wheat Beers, the list goes on and they are all there for the taking. Fashions come and fashions go, so brew what you like to drink and maybe become an expert at it.

And remember, beer is the most sociable of drinks – so have fun with friends when making it, drinking it, learning from it and laughing together with it.

Mark Tranter, Burning Sky Brewery

INTRODUCTION

The first beers I remember drinking were on family camping trips. Long before I was legally allowed to drink in the UK, my Dad would let me have a sip or two – maybe even a glass – of lager when we were in the south of France where the legal drinking age was more ambiguous. I still have a soft spot for those stubby little bottles of beer, especially ice cold on a hot day around a barbecue.

This book isn't just about how to brew your own beer: we'll also cover beer styles, a little history and the ingredients and science behind brewing. Beer is often more than a drink to people. It's a social lubricant or a way to wind down; it is something we share with friends. Memories are made when we're having a beer and our taste buds remember those moments. The next time that flavour rolls over our tongue, memories come flooding back – one sip of a cheap 25cl bottle of French lager and I'm back on a campsite, around the barbecue with family and friends.

My first pints of real ale were enjoyed in the pubs of Stourbridge, in the West Midlands, UK, but when I moved to Brighton (during my student days) I was drawn to more bargain-priced brews that were easier on my pocket. As a result of this policy, I went off beer because most of the cheap stuff wasn't very good.

At this point I started working in a brewpub, then The Font and Firkin. This was one of a chain of Firkin Brewery pubs, started by David Bruce in 1979, which were made famous by their on-site breweries. We weren't brewing much at the time, though, as the chain had been sold and there wasn't a lot of love for those beers in a 600-capacity sports and music venue. However, a chap called Mark Tranter (who went on to be head brewer for Dark Star and later start his own brewery, Burning Sky) used to don his white wellies roughly once a week just to uphold the terms of our licence. It is with some regret that I never learnt more or even showed interest in brewing at the time. Such a wasted opportunity.

My beer adventure was resurrected when I moved to London and began working at The Flask, an iconic Highgate pub. There we had a range of imported Belgian and German beers and six changing real ales – in 2003 this definitely wasn't the norm! After getting to grips with the beer range, learning to cellar beer properly and falling for Timothy Taylor's 'Landlord', Adnams 'Broadside' and Hopback's 'Summer Lightning,' I signed up for a beer and food matching event at a tiny Belgian bar in Clerkenwell called The Dovetail. It was an epiphany! I was not impressed with my first taste of sour beer, a gueuze, until I tried it with a mouthful of spicy sweet and sour prawns. What a marriage! I was hooked!

Between 2006 and 2014, while running my own pub, The Thatchers Arms, on the border of Essex and Suffolk, I brewed with lots of local brewers. I also tried my first homebrew kit, hosted regular beer dinners of my own and began writing about beer and pubs. However, I became steadily envious of the burgeoning beer scene that had erupted since I left London. In 2014 I returned to the capital and joined London Brewing Co. to head up their brewpub The Bull, which was another Highgate hostelry. I spent two years getting involved in every aspect of the north London beer haven. From brewing to branding, cellaring to serving and hosting beer events and beer and food matching evenings, it was a real treat.

In 2016 – at around the same time I started writing this book – I left The Bull to work for Borough Wines and Beers. As I write this we are in the process of starting a 1bbl (1 barrel) nanobrewery, The Brewery Below, with Dan Price as our 'Brewer in Residence.' Dan has contributed some recipes and valuable beery guidance to this book, which is a culmination of the knowledge I have gained from breweries and brewers, friends in the British Guild of Beer Writers and my own experiences and adventures in beer. I hope that it not only helps you start your own beer adventure, but that your brews bring you and your friends together to create your own long-lasting malty memories!

PLAN

What is beer and how do you make it? It's often said that brewers don't make beer, they make 'wort,' and it's yeast that makes the beer. However, there are plenty of decisions a brewer can make to influence how the yeast will carry out its part of the job.

This chapter will help you gain an understanding of the ingredients used to make beer and the influence they can have on the finished product. With just four ingredients you can produce a vast array of beer styles, with a huge variety of flavours. I would suggest you get to know beer's 'family-tree' and plan your first brew day by choosing your kit, favoured brewing method and the style of beer you want to brew.

WATER

Water is the first of four key components essential in producing beer. As well as ending up in the finished product, water is used for cleaning throughout the brewing process and is also lost through evaporation.

MASH

Water's biggest influence on the brew is while extracting sugars from the grain. This process – where grains are rested in warm water – is called 'mashing.'

DIFFERENT TYPES

The water you drink is rarely as simple as just H_2O. Water supplies vary from city to city and different water can be better suited to different styles of beer. The hardness of the water affects perceived bitterness, while the alkalinity of the water affects efficiency in beer making.

ALKALINITY

The alkalinity (pH) of the mash is determined not just by the water you use, but also the 'grist,' or grains in the mash. This means the water will have far less effect on your beer if you're extract brewing (*see page 36*), as this process has already occurred.

FOUR PINTS OF WATER ARE USED TO PRODUCE EVERY PINT OF BEER

95%
water in the
final content

WATER PROFILE BY BEER STYLE

SOFT

HARD

LOW

ALKALINITY

HIGH

WHEAT BEER

PILSNER

BRITISH BITTER

SWEET STOUT

BOCK

DARK LAGER

EXPORT LAGER

DRY STOUT

IPA

MALT

Malt is grain that has been steeped, germinated and dried, and can then be used for brewing or distilling. The most common malt is malted barley, but other grains, including rice and sorghum, can also be used. Often described as the 'backbone' of any beer, malt delivers the sugars that are needed to ferment a brew.

FLAVOUR

Malt has a huge influence on the drink's flavour, colour, body and head. Darker malts can add roasted, chocolate and coffee flavours, while amber malts bring toffee and caramel to the party. Pale malts are more delicate, but honey and biscuit notes are very common.

MALTING PROCESS

Barley kernels store sugars for the new plant as carbohydrates. During germination these carbohydrates are broken down into simpler sugars, which are just the kind you need for brewing. Essentially grains of barley are fooled into thinking it is time to grow, by making them warm and wet. In doing so, the starch in the grain is naturally converted into sugar (intended to be plant food), before the malt is kilned to stop the process.

COLOUR RANGE

Colours range from very pale lager and ale malts to darker, or even black, malts. Darker roast and speciality malts can significantly affect the colour of the beer, as well as its flavour. Only a very small amount of dark malt is required to produce a dark beer. The majority of any 'grain bill' – the ingredients used for the mash – will always be pale. This is also known as the 'base malt,' which contains more useful sugars to convert to alcohol.

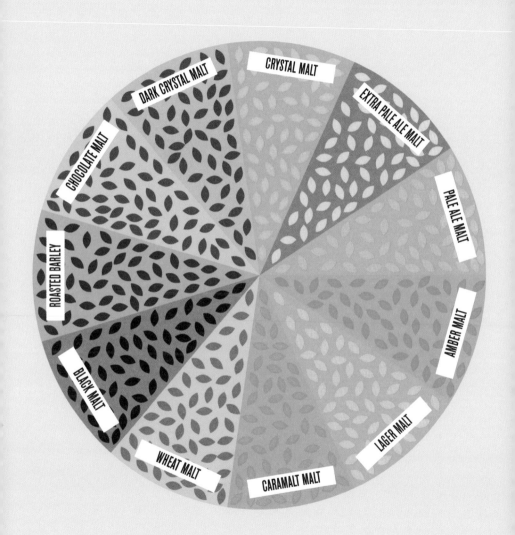

CRYSTAL MALT

DARK CRYSTAL MALT

EXTRA PALE ALE MALT

CHOCOLATE MALT

PALE ALE MALT

ROASTED BARLEY

AMBER MALT

BLACK MALT

LAGER MALT

WHEAT MALT

CARAMALT MALT

THE MALTING PROCESS

Seeds or kernels contain starch. When the plant thinks it is ready to start growing, during the germination of the seed, the starch is converted into sugar. Malting is the careful management of this process so that you stop the seed when it has the right amount of sugar for your brew. The malting process looks like this:

1. KERNELS

The raw ingredient is usually barley seeds.

2. STEEPING

The kernels are left warm and wet so they begin to germinate.

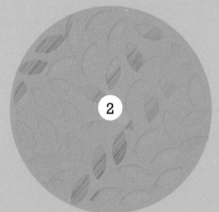

MAILLARD REACTION

Browning the malt relies on the *Maillard* reaction, which is present when searing a steak or toasting a marshmallow, and adds colour and flavour. Named after the French chemist, Louis-Camille Maillard, it is a reaction between amino acids and reducing sugars.

3. GERMINATION
Starch begins to convert to sugars.

4. KILNING
The kernels are dried; the length of time the malt is kilned or 'browned' for determines the final colour.

5. MILLING
Grinding the malt makes the sugars easier to break down.

HOPS

Hops are the female flowers – also called 'seed cones' or 'strobiles' – of the hop plant *Humulus lupulus.*

PACKING A PUNCH

Hops are to beer what seasoning is to food, and for the small proportion of the ingredients that they represent, hops can have a huge impact on the flavour of beer.

INTERNATIONAL BITTERING UNITS (IBU)

Boiling hops for at least 60 minutes converts alpha acids, found in the lupulin gland of the hop, into iso-alpha acids and creates bitterness. This bitterness is measured in International Bittering Units (IBU) and is what gives 'bitter' its name. The higher the number, the more iso-alpha acids in the beer.

HOPS: A HISTORY

Hops have been used regularly in beer since around the 12th century. However, they weren't common in British beer until the late 15th century, when brewers from the low countries of Europe brought their brewing techniques across the English channel.

IBU IN BEER TYPES

ANATOMY OF A HOP

STRIG (OR STEM)
Where the hop would have been attached to the hop bine; can impart some tannins

BRACT
The leafy part of the hop

BRACTEOLES
The inner structure of the hop cone; protects the lupulin gland; small source of oils and resins

LUPULIN GLAND
Packed with essential oils and resins to impart flavour, aroma and bitterness to beer

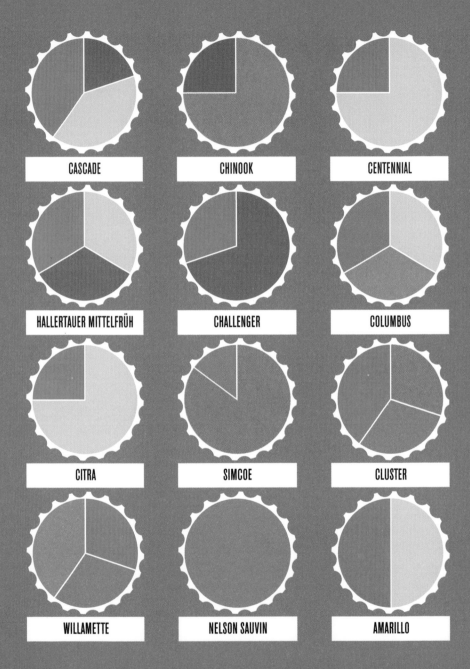

CASCADE

CHINOOK

CENTENNIAL

HALLERTAUER MITTELFRÜH

CHALLENGER

COLUMBUS

CITRA

SIMCOE

CLUSTER

WILLAMETTE

NELSON SAUVIN

AMARILLO

THE IMPORTANCE OF HOPS

As well as putting the bitterness into bitter, hops serve some other very important purposes in brewing:

Flavour: Depending on the hop variety used, boiling imparts bitterness and other characteristic flavours that balance the sweetness of malt.

Aroma: Steeping hops in beer before fermentation, or 'dry hopping' after fermentation, adds strong aromas.

Preservative: The antibiotic nature of hops, which can inhibit the growth of bacteria, helps beer last longer and stifles contamination.

Filter: Whole-leaf hops can act as a filter bed in the kettle, helping to prevent unwanted proteins, or 'trub,' getting to the fermentation.

DIFFERENT VARIETIES

Different hop varieties contain varying amounts of alpha acids and have different aromas. Much like grapes, the soil and climate in which the hops are grown has a huge impact on their characteristics. Noble hops – typically European or 'old world' – are low in bitterness, but high in aroma, so tend to be subtle and earthy. New World hops – which are usually grown in hotter climates like their 'new world' wine cousins – are bright, zingy and lively, which translates into high bitterness and aroma.

HOP FLAVOURS AND AROMAS

FLORAL

CITRUS

FRUITY

EVERGREEN

HERBAL

SPICY

EARTHY

YEAST

Yeast is a single-cell microorganism and a member of the fungus family. Although technically not an ingredient – it is generally not desirable for it to be present in a finished beer – it would be impossible to brew without it.

CULTIVATED YEAST

As late as the 19th century, people didn't really understand how beer became alcoholic, but that soon changed. Thanks to the outstanding work of French microbiologist, Louis Pasteur, by the end of the 19th century, two strains of brewing yeast had been identified, *Saccharomyces cerevisiae* and *Saccharomyces carlsbergensis* (later renamed *Saccharomyces pastorianus*). The most common brewing yeasts in use today have been cultivated.

WILD YEAST

Some wild yeasts are also used to ferment beer, usually resulting in a tart, sour taste. These wild yeasts can be far less predictable, but the Belgians in particular have embraced this. The result, when done properly, is often a beautifully complex beer.

CALIFORNIA ALE
Clean, neutral yeast; great for most styles of beer.

BELGIAN WIT
Adds some sweetness; is spicy and has phenolic or medicinal aromas.

SAISON
Produces a dry, tart beer with plenty of phenols.

BELGIAN ALE
Ferments to high strength's leaving a fruity character.

GERMAN HEFEWEIZEN
Used in wheat beers; adds aromas of banana and clove.

PILSNER
Dry yeast with a malty finish.

BRITISH ALE
Enhances the malt character of a beer.

HOW YEAST WORKS

Yeast enables the production of alcohol through fermentation. The sugar in the hopped wort – the sugary liquid made during the mash – is converted to carbon dioxide (CO_2) and alcohol, while the yeast itself multiplies by cell division or 'budding.'

Brettanomyces is a wild yeast that could now be considered domesticated due to its common use and deliberate inoculation in some beers. 'Brett' is found on the skins of fruit in the wild and can be harboured in wood, often 'infecting' beers stored in wooden barrels.

GERMAN KÖLSCH
Clean with a touch of honey; helps accentuate hop flavours.

LACTOBACILLUS
A wild yeast used for sour beers.

BRETTANOMYCES
Dry, smoky, spicy and sour.

BEER CATEGORIES

LAGER

Derived from the German word 'to store,' lagers are historically brewed in the winter months and stored in cool cellars or caves to be drunk throughout the summer. Lagers are fermented with *Saccharomyces pastorianus*, which prefers cooler temperatures. Traditionally, a lager would be aged for around 20–90 days, although many modern mainstream lagers forgo this 'lagering' or ageing process.

SACCHAROMYCES PASTORIANUS

A bottom-fermenting yeast, used to produce lagers. Ferments at lower temperatures of around 50°F (10°C).

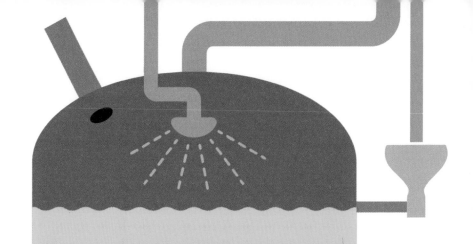

ALE

Defined by the type of yeast used, ales are generally produced with *Saccharomyces cerevisiae*, which lives and reproduces on the top of the fermenting beer. This makes it easy to harvest excess yeast for further brewing, but can also leave the yeast vulnerable to spoilage or contamination from wild airborne yeast strains.

WILD BEER

Brewed with wild yeasts, often from the natural surroundings of the brewery, these beers tend to be sour, tart and complex. Belgian lambic beers use airborne yeasts, while 'Brett' beers rely on yeast found on fruit and in wooden casks during the ageing process.

SACCHAROMYCES CEREVISIAE

A top-fermenting yeast, used to produce ales. Ferments at warm temperatures in the region of 64.4°F (18°C).

BEER STYLES

LAGERS

PILSNER
The original golden lager from the Czech town of Pilsen; a biscuity malt with a clean, grassy bitterness.

HELLES
A pale, soft German style of lager; lighter in colour and intensity than Pilsner.

VIENNA
Amber lager with a toffee and caramel sweetness, toasted notes and low bitterness.

CALIFORNIA COMMON
A lager fermented at ale temperatures; usually a Vienna-style lager with fruity notes. Also known as steam beer.

WILD BEERS

DARK LAGER

Known as *Schwarzbier* in Germany. Jet black opaque beer with coffee and chocolate notes.

BOCK

A strong, German style of lager usually – but not exclusively – dark in colour, with a malty taste.

DOPPELBOCK

A stronger, maltier version of the bock.

LAMBIC

Spontaneously fermented using wild yeasts; tart, sour and earthy.

GUEUZE

A blend of 1-year-old and 2–3-year-old lambics; the skill of the blender is vital to this style.

KRIEK / FRAMBOISE

Traditionally, a lambic Belgian brown ale aged with added cherries (Kriek) or raspberries (Framboise).

BEER STYLES

BRITISH BITTER
Traditional English ales are well hopped, hence the term 'bitter.'

ESB (EXTRA SPECIAL BITTER)
Maltier, fruitier and stronger than a best bitter.

AMERICAN RED/BROWN
A US take on British red and brown ales with generous amounts of American hops.

PALE ALE
A paler version of a British bitter, sometimes as light as a lager.

IPA
Stronger, hoppier version of a pale ale, named after its historical association with the long voyage from Britain to India.

BARLEY WINE
Strong, sweet malty beer; 'wine' reflects the strength of the beverage rather than the flavour or the ingredients.

STOUT/PORTER

Dark beer with coffee and chocolate notes. Originally two styles, but opinions have become mixed over time.

IMPERIAL STOUT

A dark stout originally exported to Russia to impress the Czar; dark fruity with high residual sugars.

MILD

A misunderstood style. Originally 'fresh' ale, but now represented by often dark, mildly hopped and usually low strength British beer.

WHEAT

From the German Hefeweizen to Belgian Wit, a wheat beer can be dark or golden, but has a healthy addition of wheat to the 'mash bill.'

BERLINER WEISSE

From Germany, a wheat beer that undergoes a lactic (sour) fermentation. Sweetened with syrups.

SAISON

The farmhouse style of beer of 'the season,' brewed using a now-domesticated wild yeast.

KÖLSCH

Only brewed in Cologne, Germany. A very pale ale that is then lagered; delicate with a honey sweetness.

BEER FAMILY TREE

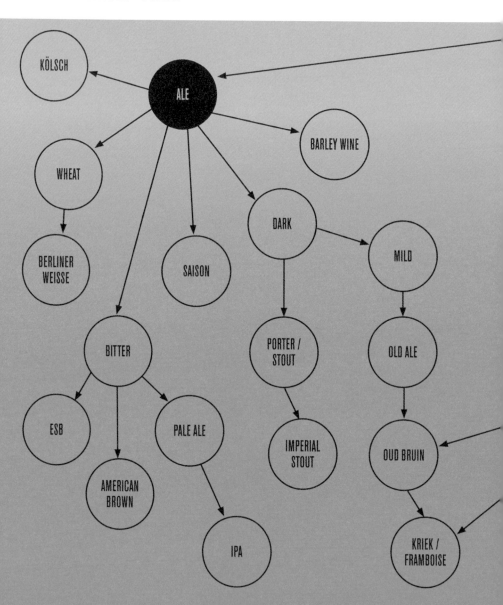

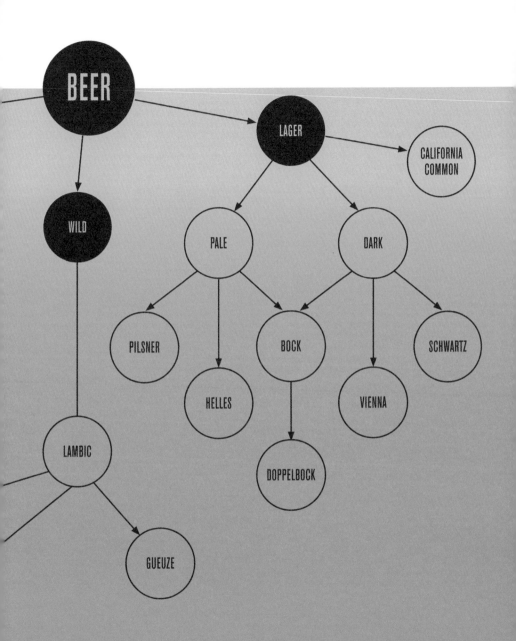

HOMEBREW EQUIPMENT

6-GALLON BOILING POT

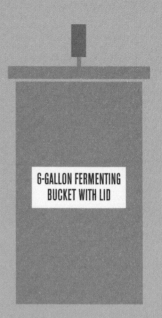

6-GALLON FERMENTING BUCKET WITH LID

2 YARDS (2M) FOOD GRADE PIPE / BEER LINE

BREWING SPOON OR SLOTTED PADDLE

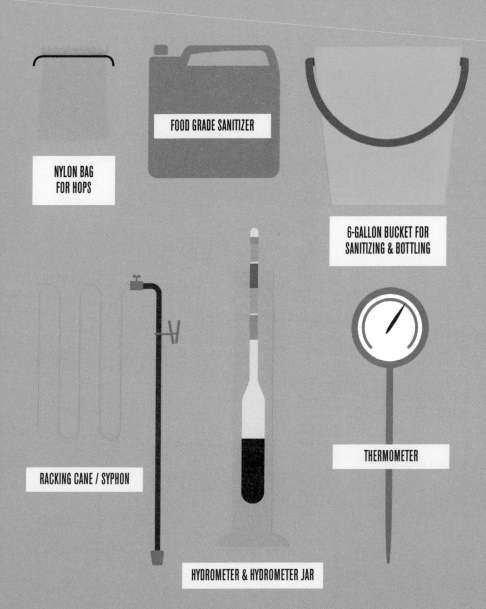

NYLON BAG
FOR HOPS

FOOD GRADE SANITIZER

6-GALLON BUCKET FOR
SANITIZING & BOTTLING

RACKING CANE / SYPHON

THERMOMETER

HYDROMETER & HYDROMETER JAR

FOR STORAGE

BOTTLING WAND

BOTTLE CAPS

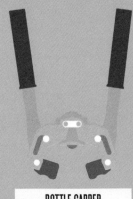

BOTTLE CAPPER

UPGRADES

MASH TUN (FOR ALL GRAIN BREWING)

BREW BOILER

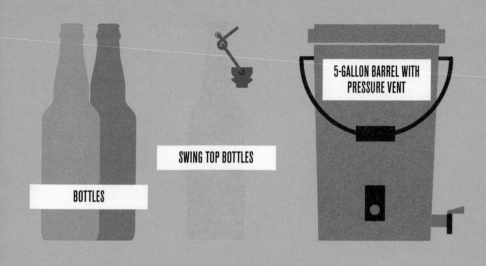

BOTTLES

SWING TOP BOTTLES

5-GALLON BARREL WITH PRESSURE VENT

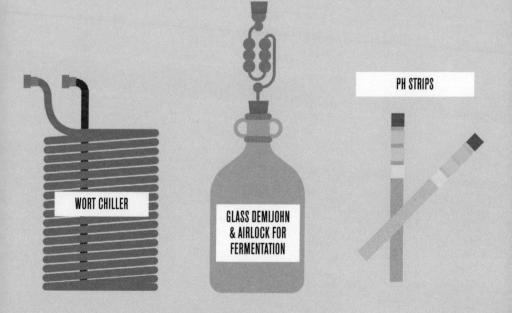

WORT CHILLER

GLASS DEMIJOHN & AIRLOCK FOR FERMENTATION

PH STRIPS

EXTRACT BREWING

There are two main approaches to home brewing: extract brewing and all grain brewing. Of the two, extract brewing is the simplest and most common for beginners. In this process, water is added to malt extract and boiled; hops are added; the beer is then cooled and fermented. This method removes the need for the mash, which is the first – and more complex – step of all grain brewing.

1. BOIL
Water is added to malt extract and the resultant wort is boiled.

2. ADD HOPS
This produces the bitterness and aroma, as per the recipe.

3. COOL
The hopped wort is cooled to 68°F (20°C).

BREW KITS

Malt extracts of well-known beer brands can be purchased already made. Coopers, an Australian craft brewer, and Woodforde's, a traditional British brewer, both make a range of popular beer kits. Individual malt extracts are also available to buy, so you can blend them for your own recipes. For example, Coopers produces a range of malt extracts from pale through to amber and dark; the pale should be used as a base with small amounts of darker, roasted extracts for colour and flavour. More adventurous extract brewers can try steeping speciality malt grains in their base extract to add a little more body to the final beer.

4. ADD YEAST
Once the beer is chilled, the yeast can be added.

5. FERMENT
The yeast converts sugar into CO_2 and alcohol.

6. BOTTLE
Package your beer and store it before drinking.

ALL GRAIN BREWING

Brewers around the world use all grain brewing for most commercial beers, albeit on a large scale. It gets its name because the process starts with grains – usually malted barley – instead of already formulated wort or malt extract.

All grain brewing is more involved and requires a little more discipline than extract brewing, as there are more opportunities to make mistakes that can affect the quality of your beer. It is also slightly more expensive, as you'll need some extra brew kit – a mash tun for a start – and your brew day will be at least an hour longer. However, in return you will have far more control over the beer and far more freedom to produce a greater variety of styles.

THE PROCESS

1. HEAT
A water temperature of around 155°F (68°C) is ideal for a medium-bodied beer, but anywhere in the region of 145–167°F (63–75°C) will work.

2. MASH
Add crushed grains of malted barley and steep to extract sugars. The temperature and water profile have a significant effect on the beer, so precision is key when 'mashing in.'

3. SPARGE
Warm water is added to the mash and recirculated to rinse the grains and maximize the extract.

4. WORT
The sugary water, produced by steeping grain in hot water, is influenced by the temperature and pH of the mash.

5. BOIL
The resultant wort is boiled.

6. COOL
The hopped wort is cooled to 68°F (20°C).

7. ADD HOPS
This produces the bitterness and aroma.

8. ADD YEAST
Once the beer is chilled, the yeast can be added.

9. FERMENT
The yeast converts sugar into CO_2 and alcohol.

10. BOTTLE
Package your beer and store it before drinking.

MAKE

With a solid understanding of beer styles and brewing you should have an idea of what you might like to brew. This chapter will walk you through the brew day itself so you can prepare your kit and enjoy a successful brew.

Many people draw parallels between brewers and chefs, as both use their imagination to bring flavours together. However, brewers are perhaps more closely aligned to pastry chefs: creativity is important, but it plays second fiddle to the science and precision needed for a good result. Whether you're brewing from your first extract kit or you're an accomplished brewer experimenting with your own all grain recipes, the process doesn't alter much. The control points are the same, and just as critical.

Your first brew day is likely to be a full day, so allow plenty of time and start early. Once you're well-practised, things should be quicker and you will probably be able to get everything done and cleaned up within 5–6 hours at most. As with any project, planning and preparation will stand you in good stead, so make a checklist and run through everything before you begin.

BREW DAY CHECKLIST

SUGAR

WATER

YEAST

MALT

HOPS

2 YARDS (2M) FOOD GRADE PIPE / BEER LINE

NYLON BAG FOR HOPS

THERMOMETER

SANITIZER

6-GALLON BUCKET FOR SANITIZING & BOTTLING

HYDROMETER & HYDROMETER JAR

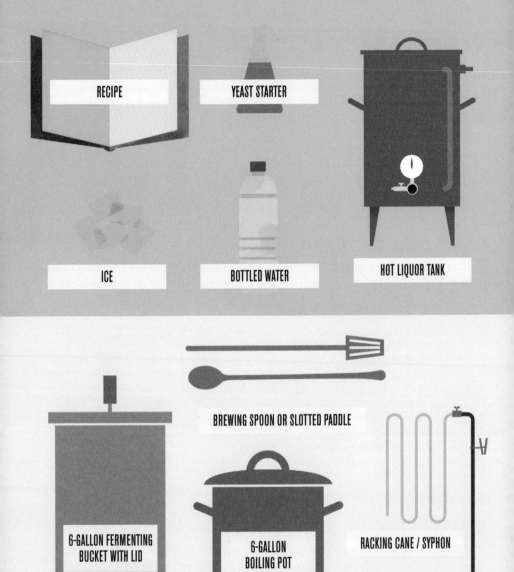

RECIPE

YEAST STARTER

ICE

BOTTLED WATER

HOT LIQUOR TANK

BREWING SPOON OR SLOTTED PADDLE

6-GALLON FERMENTING BUCKET WITH LID

6-GALLON BOILING POT

RACKING CANE / SYPHON

BEFORE YOU BEGIN

DAY BEFORE

CHECK THE RECIPE AGAINST THE INGREDIENTS

 EQUIPMENT IS CLEANED AND ACCOUNTED FOR

ICE IN FREEZER FOR CHILLING THE WORT

 WATER IN HOT LIQUOR TANK

SANITIZER BOTTLE FULL

 YEAST STARTER READY (OPTIONAL)

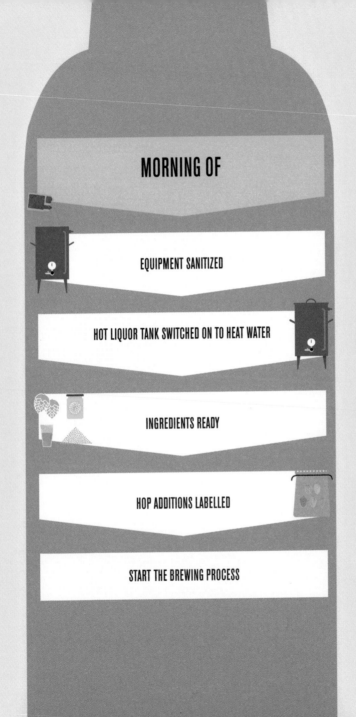

MORNING OF

EQUIPMENT SANITIZED

HOT LIQUOR TANK SWITCHED ON TO HEAT WATER

INGREDIENTS READY

HOP ADDITIONS LABELLED

START THE BREWING PROCESS

CLEANING

DON'T FORGET
You will need to sanitize all of your bottling or kegging equipment and containers before packaging your finished product.

Most commercial brewers – successful ones at any rate – will tell you that brewing is '90% cleaning.' The most important items are those that come into contact with the beer after it has boiled. Although boiling will sanitize the brew and kill any infections picked up before reaching the kettle, that's no reason to relax. Infections from a dirty brewpot or mash tun are unlikely, but unwanted flavours can be imparted, especially from a burnt or caramelized kettle. You should make sure you clean your mash tun, brewpot, kettle and brewing spoon.

SANITIZING

A sanitizer (or sterilizer) will kill any bacteria that is likely to spoil your wort or infect your yeast. Most commercial brewers use peracetic acid. This is because the sanitizer doesn't need rinsing, which avoids anything that might cause infection – water, for example, can carry an array of nasties. There are also 'non-rinse,' food-safe sanitizers more readily available for homebrewers, such as *Star San*. Whatever you decide to use, be sure to sanitize everything.

ACCURACY IS KEY

When the brew day arrives, you should have made your final preparations and be ready to brew. These next pages will walk you through the steps involved and help you to avoid any of the common pitfalls.

CALIBRATING A PROBE
It is important to be accurate when brewing and this is especially important with temperatures. You should calibrate your temperature probe regularly to ensure that it is giving you accurate readings.

LOWEST TEMPERATURE
1. Prepare a mix of cold water and ice, and leave it to stand for a few minutes for the water to cool properly.
2. Immerse the probe in the water.
3. Your reading should be 32°F (0°C).

HIGHEST TEMPERATURE
1. Bring a pot of water to the boil.
2. After the water has been boiling for a few minutes, reset the probe and immerse it in the water.
3. Your reading should be 212°F (100°C).

TROUBLESHOOTING
If either of your readings is different to the values above, your probe potentially needs calibrating. Repeat the test, taking care not to touch the side of the vessel containing the water, as this could cause an erroneous measurement. If you get the same (incorrect) reading(s) then follow the probe's manual to adjust it.

YEAST PREPARATION

If you're brewing regularly you should always have a source of yeast at the ready. However, if you're brewing less frequently you'll need to prepare a yeast 'starter' and it's recommended that you do this before you even get your brew kit out. Without yeast you won't be able to ferment.

DRY YEAST

Dry yeast is ideal for the novice brewer, as packets have a long shelf life and contain plenty of viable yeast cells. It is always best to have a backup, though, and the yeast should ideally be rehydrated before you add it to your wort.

THE PROCESS

1. WARM WATER
Put 250ml (9fl oz) of warm, previously boiled, water in a sanitized jug. The temperature should be about 85°F (30°C).

2. ADD YEAST
Add two packets of dry yeast and cover with plastic wrap or cling film.

GODISGOOD

Before yeast was identified as a microorganism, brewers still knew it was vital to making beer. They may not have understood what is was, or how it worked, but they knew how important it was and called it 'godisgood.' They would harvest yeast from a previous brew and add it to the wort they wanted to ferment, and this is something you can still do today.

3. BUBBLES
If there aren't any signs of bubbling within 30 minutes, your yeast is probably dead.

4. PROOF
Proof the yeast by adding 1 teaspoon of malt extract or sugar that has been boiled in water (and then cooled).

5. COMPLETE
After 30 minutes it should be lively, foaming and ready to pitch.

THE PROCESS

1. ADD WATER

Fill your pot (mash tun)
with 1 litre of water for
every 500g (17.6 oz) of malt.

2. HEAT

Heat the water until it reaches
around 160–165°F (70–73°C).

3. ADD MALT BILL

Add your malt bill from your
recipe; the temperature should
drop to around 150–155°F
(65–68°C).

MASH

If you are using all grain brewing then you will need to mash. The mash is where sugars are extracted from crushed malted grains by adding warm water. Steeping the malt at specific temperatures activates enzymes that break down the barley into the sugars the yeast will need to ferment.

4. MAINTAIN TEMPERATURE

Maintain the temperature as close to 155°F (68°C) as you can for one hour.

5. STIR

Stir gently every 10 minutes, taking regular temperature readings. Use a lid to maintain the temperature.

6. HEAT AND COOL

After one hour, increase the heat to 170°F (77°C), stirring constantly to avoid burning. Once you reach this, take off the heat and cool: you have 'mashed out' and are ready to begin 'the sparge.'

SPARGE

Sparging, sometimes reffered to as 'lautering,' occurs at the end of the mash. It is a process that continually moistens and rinses the grain with warm water to help extract as much fermentable sugar as possible. The temperature at which you extract these sugars can have a huge impact on the quality of your wort. Ideally you want to keep the mash at around 150–160°F (65–70°C). There are two common sparge methods: a continual, or 'fly' sparge, and a batch sparge, shown below.

THE PROCESS

1. ADD WATER

To start with you need to know how much water you added to your mash (see step 1 of 'The Mash Process' on page 52) and have at least the same amount of water available, at a temperature of around 160°F (70°C).

2. SET THE MASH BED

Draw a single jug of wort at a time off the bottom and pour it over the mash until it runs clear. At this point the mash bed is set, so you shouldn't get any particles in your kettle.

CONTINUAL SPARGE

Continual sparging takes around 60–90 minutes, with warm water sprinkled over the top of the grain as it is drained into the kettle. The process requires careful temperature control and the equipment can be costly, but it is usually the most efficient method.

BATCH SPARGE

Batch sparging is recommend for most people starting out, as it is quicker than continual sparging and requires less attention and kit. However, it is around 5% less efficient, so you will require more grain to begin with.

3. DRAIN

Drain the wort into your kettle.

4. RESET THE MASH BED

Measure how much wort you have drained into the kettle. Add the additional amount of water required to your mash and repeat step 2 to reset the mash bed.

5. REPEAT

Again, drain the wort into your kettle. If necessary, repeat steps 3 and 4 until you have the required amount of wort.

BOIL

The boil is essential for sterilizing the wort and is the point at which the all grain and extract brewing methods converge. There are, however, subtle differences between the two processes.

HOW LONG TO BOIL FOR?

With all grain brewing, hops are added. The hop character you want for your beer will determine how much hops you add and when you add it. Most bittering hops require a boil of one hour to fully utilize the alpha acids from the hops. In all grain brewing this boil time also helps coagulate proteins and boil off any unwanted volatiles that can create 'off flavours.' In extract brewing you only need to boil for as long as the longest hop addition, as per your recipe.

1. BOIL
Bring your wort to the boil and note the start time.

2. FIRST ADDITION
Make your first hop addition.

ADDITION TIME

When you are extract brewing add your hops straight away, but for all grain brewing you need to take the time of the first addition away from 60 minutes to calculate when to add them. For example, if you have a 20 minute addition, that should be added 40 minutes after the start of the boil.

HOT BREAK

As your wort boils it will start to foam as the proteins coagulate; this is known as the 'hot break' and is a good sign that indicates a clearer beer! To prevent your wort from boiling over, either spray with cool water or turn down the heat. The addition of hops may also encourage a hot break.

3. ADDITIONAL HOPS

Continue to time your boil and add your hops at the relevant points.

4. IRISH MOSS

Add Irish moss 15 minutes before the end of boil (and usually with a hop addition). This is a form of dried seaweed that will help clump the proteins together, giving a clearer beer.

5. FINAL ADDITION

Add your final aroma hop additions in the final five minutes of boiling, or even at 'flameout' when you turn off the heat.

STEEP & COOL

After the boil, some recipes may require you to steep your hops. Much like brewing tea, this simply means leaving the hops in the hot wort to increase the efficiency and extract.

AROMA & BITTERNESS

Any hops added towards the end of the brew will be adding aroma, so the longer contact time the liquid has, the more aroma will transfer to the beer. However, at high temperatures the alpha acids in hops convert to bitterness, so there is a fine line between aroma and bitterness.

THE PROCESS

1. STEEP HOPS

Steep your hops in hot wort, stirring occasionally using a sanitized spoon. Leave the boil kettle lid on for maximum effect.

After the boil your beer will be susceptible to infection, so anything that your beer comes into contact with should be sterilized from now on.

2. DRAIN BEER

Remove the hops by taking your 'hop sock' out, or – if you didn't use one – drain the beer to a different vessel.

20°c

3. COOL

Cool the beer to just under 70°F (20°C) as quickly as possible, ideally using a sterilized wort chiller.

4. TRANSFER BEER

Transfer the cooled beer to your fermentation vessel. Oxygen (O_2) in your wort will help the yeast activate, so it is helpful to aerate your wort at this point. Either stir it vigorously before transfer, or 'drip' your wort through a sieve during the transfer.

ORIGINAL GRAVITY

Before you can add the yeast – a process known as 'pitching' – you need to know your wort's original gravity, which is a measure of how much sugar it contains. The original gravity is determined using a hydrometer, which measures the density of the wort. Comparing this measurement to that of water tells you how much sugar is present. Once you know how much sugar is present you can estimate how much the yeast will convert to alcohol, giving you an idea of the final strength, or gravity, of your beer.

CALIBRATING THE HYDROMETER

When placed in water at 68°F (20°C) a hydrometer should read 1000. Calibrate your hydrometer by placing it in the water you use to brew with at 68°F (20°C). If the reading isn't 1000, then you either need to make an adjustment to your final reading, or get a new hydrometer!

USING THE HYDROMETER

1. Take a sample of your wort and float the hydrometer in it.
2. Where the liquid rises to on your hydrometer is your original gravity reading.

Once you have an original gravity you can measure the progress of your yeast by taking further readings during fermentation (see pages 64–65), although it is important that this is done carefully, with sterile equipment.

CORRECT READING —————————————————— INCORRECT READING

HYDROMETER READINGS

While there are charts to calculate readings taken at different temperatures, it is simpler to always take them at 68°F (20°C). If the temperatue is higher or lower than this, you can calculate the difference by using the table below.

°F	°C	G CHANGE
59	15	-0.0010
60.8	16	-0.0008
62.6	17	-0.0006
64.4	18	-0.0004
66.2	19	-0.0002
68	20	0
69.8	21	0.0002
71.6	22	0.0004
73.4	23	0.0006
75.2	24	0.0008
77	25	0.0010
78.8	26	0.0012
80.6	27	0.0014
82.4	28	0.0016
84.2	29	0.0018
86	30	0.0020
87.8	31	0.0022
89.6	32	0.0024
91.4	33	0.0026
93.2	34	0.0028
95	35	0.0030
96.8	36	0.0032
98.6	37	0.0034

PITCH

Once your wort is cool you are ready to add, or 'pitch,' your yeast to begin the fermentation stage. Your 'pitching rate' is the number of active yeast cells you need to add to a batch; getting this wrong can result in long lag times or fermentation problems.

HOW MUCH YEAST SHOULD YOU ADD?

Homebrew shops sell yeast in sachets, usually for a 5-gallon pitch, and one pack of hydrated yeast is the ideal amount. This is just a guideline, though, and different recipes may call for different amounts – stronger beers may require additional yeast, for example.

TEMPERATURE

Yeast likes to be added at 68°F (20°C), but pitching at cooler temperatures (64.4–66.3°F / 18–19°C) will produce cleaner flavours, and pitching at slightly warmer temperatures (69.8–73.4°F / 21–23°C) will usually produce fruitier aromas. However, if the wort is too hot it will kill the yeast; too cold and it won't activate. Once you have reached the desired temperature for your pitch you can add your active yeast to the beer.

ABV

As the yeast turns the sugar into alcohol your hydrometer readings will decrease. The amount of sugar that converts to alcohol is an indication of the final Alcohol By Volume (ABV) of your beer.

$$\% \text{ ABV} = \frac{\text{ORIGINAL GRAVITY} - \text{FINAL GRAVITY}}{7.36} \times 1000$$

PRIMARY FERMENTATION

Primary fermentation is the conversion of the 'simple' sugars that are easy to ferment. You will yield far more consistent results at this stage if you are able to keep your brew at a steady temperature of around 64.4–71.6°F (18–22°C). This means keeping it out of direct sunlight in a location that maintains a consistent temperature and is easily accessible.

SEALED

With your yeast pitched you should seal your fermentation vessel and add an airlock. This allows excess CO_2 to be released without infection getting in. Bubbling in the airlock can also signal active primary fermentation.

WHEN IS IT READY?

To know when your brew's ready you will need to check your hydrometer readings. When fermentation is complete your original gravity should be around one quarter of what you started with. For example, an original gravity of 1.040 should reduce to around 1.010 (.010 being a quarter of .040). Depending on the yeast, the temperature and the beer, this can take anywhere from three days to two weeks. To reduce the chance of infection by repeatedly opening the fermenter to take samples, many homebrewers leave things for a standard two weeks.

STOPPING FERMENTATION

If fermentation stops, then you have reached your final gravity. However, if you reach your target gravity before fermentation stops you may want to stop the yeast by cooling the beer to 41°F (5°C), at which point the yeast becomes inactive.

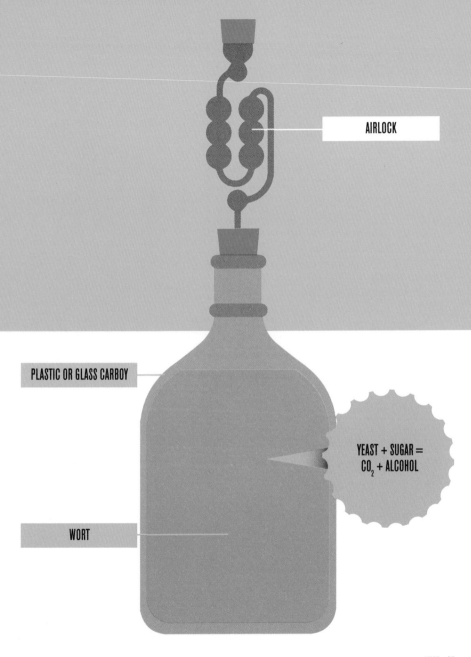

AIRLOCK

PLASTIC OR GLASS CARBOY

YEAST + SUGAR =
CO_2 + ALCOHOL

WORT

ADVANCED TECHNIQUES

SECONDARY FERMENTATION

Secondary fermentation happens when you transfer your beer after the lively primary fermentation and take it away from the dead yeast cells lying at the bottom. Transferring beer is prone to infection, though, so be careful and sanitize everything. To limit the number of transfers you have to make, secondary fermentation can happen in the bottle or in your serving keg, but it is still only recommended for more experienced brewers.

DRY HOPPING

Dry hopping is used in some recipes to enhance hop aroma, and it can also add a little bitterness. Towards the end of the fermentation process – or even post fermentation – extra hops are added to the beer. These slowly drop through the beer over the course of a few days, adding a more complex and intense aroma.

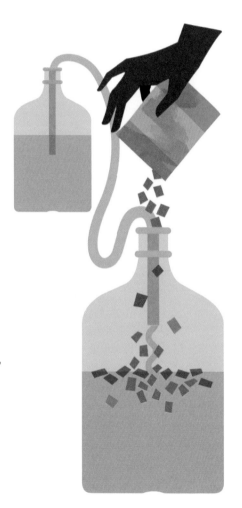

AUTOLYSIS

Leaving your beer on dead or inactive yeast for long periods of time can cause unpleasant 'off flavours' to develop through a process called 'autolysis.' This is essentially the self-destruction of unhealthy, or dying, yeast cells, which rupture and affect the flavour of the beer. Autolysis usually imparts 'umami' flavours like Marmite® (itself a yeast extract), burnt rubber or soy sauce. While this can add complexity to some stronger, dark, aged beers, it is generally considered unpleasant.

1. SANITIZE

Sanitize your bottles,
caps, syphoning hose
and bottling wand.

2. BOIL

Boil priming sugar in a
little water to sanitize it.

3. BOILING BUCKET METHOD OR FERMENTATION VESSEL METHOD

If you are using a bottling bucket, add priming sugar to it.
Carefully transfer your beer to the bucket, taking care not to
splash and add O_2 to it. You can then fill your bottles from
the tap in the bottom of the bucket using your bottle filler
before moving on to step 5. If you aren't using a bottling bucket,
add the priming sugar to the fermentation vessel and stir the
beer gently. Leave it for 30 minutes to settle.

4. FILL BOTTLES

Insert the sanitized bottle filler
into your bottle, ensuring it
goes all the way to the bottom
of the bottle. Siphon the beer
gently at first, keeping the fill
tube below the waterline to
avoid aeration.

STORAGE & CONDITIONING

Once your beer has fermented you have to decide how to store it. To start with you should use bottles. Bottling is easiest, has the lowest initial expense and it allows you to share your beers with friends, family and other brewers more easily. As you develop your brewing hobby you could consider storing your beer in kegs or in cans.

PRIMING SUGAR

Most brewers add priming sugar to their brew when they bottle. This is an extra bit of 'food' for the yeast, which should further condition the beer in the bottle and create extra CO_2. To calculate how much you should add, use the website: www.tastybrew.com/calculators/priming.html.

5. SEAL

Place a cap on the bottle and seal with a capper – this can be done in batches to save time.

6. CONDITION

Your beers should be stored somewhere warm (around 59–68°F / 15–20°C) for up to two weeks to encourage conditioning.

7. STORE

After conditioning your bottles should be placed somewhere dark and cool until you are ready to drink!

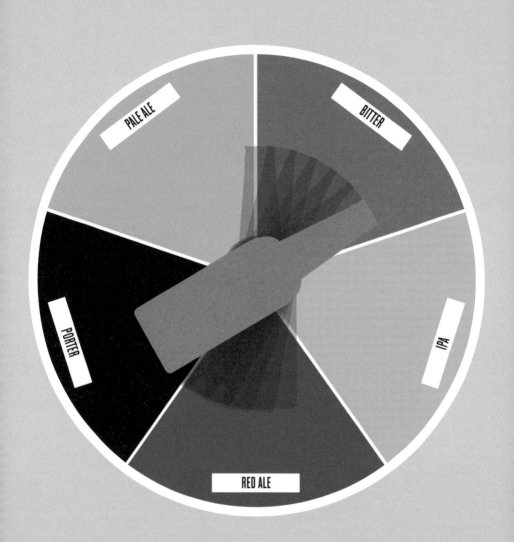

PLAY

Hopefully by this stage you've brewed a beer that you have been able to enjoy drinking as well (or are at least ready to get started). I would recommend brewing the same recipe a few times so you can monitor any differences between batches and improve your consistency. Tasting the results of different brew days next to each other can be extremely helpful, especially if you have kept notes on your brews.

Inconsistencies can lead to unusual flavours or differences in the flavour, strength or colour of your beer. This chapter will help you learn common 'off flavours' so you can identify and avoid them. There are also some all grain recipes for you to follow for common beer styles that I hope you'll enjoy brewing.

FLAVOUR WHEEL

Flavour in beer can usually be attributed to the four key ingredients – yeast, malt, hops and water – and the processes used; subtle changes in either can have a distinct influence on the final flavour.

OFF FLAVOURS

The four flavour wheels shown here highlight flavours that are most often considered to be 'off flavours,' but some can be acceptable in certain beer styles or in low volumes (just as some 'good' flavours wouldn't be welcome in certain styles).

DEVELOPING YOUR PALETTE

Using these flavour wheels should help you develop your palette and identify where any problem flavours come from. In turn this will enable you to hone your technique and improve the final flavours of your beers. However, it's important to appreciate that flavour is subjective, and your likes and dislikes can be influenced by memories of things you've tasted in the past.

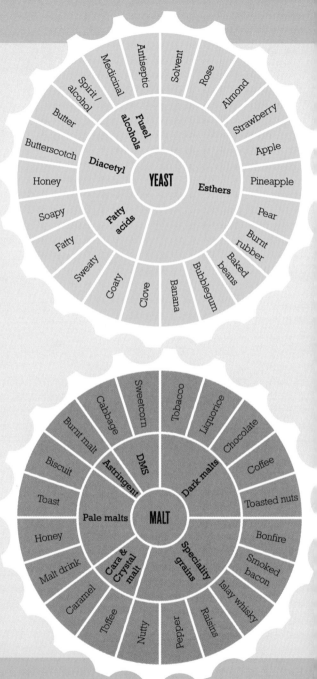

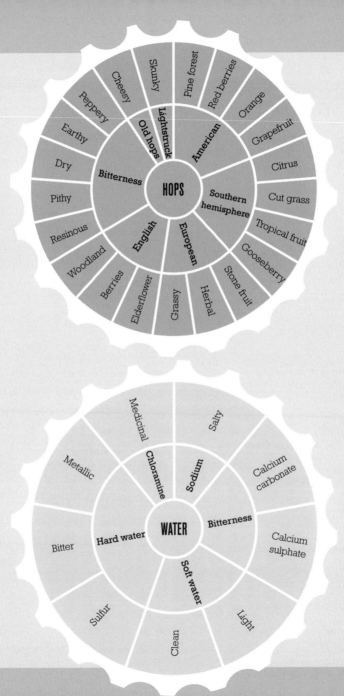

IDENTIFYING OFF FLAVOURS

ACETALDEHYDE

Tastes and smells like green apples; sharp and cidery. Small amounts can be acceptable in light lagers, but it is usually undesirable. It can be caused by a prematurely ended fermentation, oxidization or a bacteria known as *acetobactor*.

DIACETYL

Buttery, butterscotch or honey flavours are the prominent signals for this all too common fault, although small amounts are acceptable – and can even be pleasant – in some ales or pilsners. Haste is usually the culprit, so always give your beer enough time before racking. Poor yeast health or bacterial infection can also cause diacetyl to be present.

ALCOHOL

Alcohol is always present after fermentation, but too much can leave a beer tasting hot, spicy or vinous. In strong ales and lagers this is expected, but it can become present or even too dominant in lower ABV beers. High fermentation temperatures, too many fermentable sugars or not enough yeast pitched are all common causes.

ASTRINGENCY

This is never pleasant in a beer and most commonly occurs due to poor sanitation. That said, excessive use of hops, a high water pH or a high sparge temperature can also be to blame, so be careful not to boil your mash and grains.

BUTERIC ACID

Usually described as 'baby sick,' this 'off flavour' is never desirable and is usually caused by infection in the wort, or in any caramel or syrup added before fermentation.

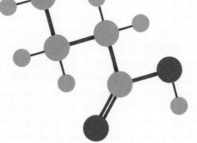

IDENTIFYING OFF FLAVOURS

DIMETHYL SULFIDE (DMS)

A vegetal flavour, often described as cooked corn or cabbage. Some people are far more susceptible to noticing this fault than others. It usually occurs through poor sanitation or sparging at too low a temperature at the mashing stage. However, a short boil or poor yeast health can have the same result. It can also be a deliberate result of the malting process in some mainstream lagers.

PHENOLS

Medicinal aromas, cloves, sticking plaster and plastic or smoky smells are the classic tells here. This is usually a wild yeast infection caused by poor sanitation, but it can also be introduced by chlorophenols in the water (these can be removed with a simple charcoal filter before brewing).

SOURNESS

Tart and sour flavours are appropriate in some Belgian and lambic styles of beer, but most often they are unwanted. Bacteria such as *Pediococcus* and *Lactobacillus* can occur through poor sanitation, but high fermentation temperatures or a mash of more than two hours can also be a motivating factor.

OXIDIZATION

Usually a sign of old or stale beer, this can be magnified by too much O_2 coming into contact with hot wort. Excessive oxidization can cause a beer to become sherry like, or even reminiscent of soy sauce.

IMPROVING CONSISTENCY

If your brews are consistent, your beer should be too, so try and ensure that you follow the same key steps throughout your brew day and during fermentation.

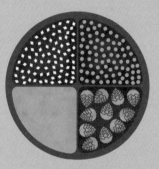

IRISH MOSS
Use Irish moss at the end of the boil stage to give a clearer beer.

FRESH INGREDIENTS
Use fresh ingredients; old hops and stale or damp malt can cause problems.

ACCURACY
Weigh your ingredients accurately.

HEALTHY YEAST
Use fresh, healthy yeast and make a good starter up to three days before brewing.

PH

Measure the pH of your water and adjust it to hit a pH of 5.2 in your mash.

TEMPERATURE

Calibrate your thermometer regularly to ensure an accurate mash temperature.

Maintain a consistent temperature throughout fermentation.

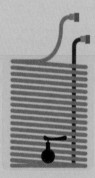

KEEP IT COOL

Cool your wort quickly; it is worth investing in a wort chiller for this.

TIME KEEPING

Good time keeping means you don't mash for too long or boil for too short a time. Ideally you should use the exact same mash and boil times for every brew.

CLEANLINESS

Sanitation should be maintained throughout the process, especially post boil when the beer is susceptible to infection.

WATER LEVELS

Measure your water using a well-marked vessel or buy a flow meter.

BEST BITTER

BEER STREET

LONDON BREWING CO.
4% ABV

I worked for London Brewing Co. for two years and 'Beer Street' was a staple of our brewpub bars and a firm favourite with locals. It's a classic brown English bitter with a crisp finish, named after the William Hogarth print of the same name.

Recipe: Adapted by Head Brewer, Rich White

BASICS

VOLUME	5 gallons (20L)
BOIL VOLUME	6.6 gallons (25L)
ABV	4.0%
TARGET FG	1011
TARGET OG	1042
PH	8.3

METHOD AND TIMINGS

MASH	
Temperature	**Time**
152°F (66°C)	60 min.

FERMENTATION
64°F (18°C)

INGREDIENTS

MALT	
Pale	5.5lb (2.5kg)
Wheat malt	8.82oz (0.25kg)
Crystal	8.82oz (0.25kg)
Chocolate malt	1.05oz (0.03kg)

HOPS			
	Weight	Addition time	Attribute
Goldings	0.94oz (26.67g)	60 min.	Bittering
Fuggles	1.47oz (41.67g)	9 min.	Aroma

YEAST
S-04 SafAle English Ale

BREWERS' TIP
To bring out the best in these British hops, Burtonize your water. Burtonization is the process of changing the profile of your water to match that of Burton-on-Trent. Ask your water supplier for a profile of your water before adding any salts.

PALE ALE

CITRA PALE ALE

BREWERY BELOW
4.3–4.8% ABV

At the time of writing this I work for Borough Wines & Beers. We are currently installing a 1-barrel nano brewery, The Brewery Below, in a bank vault beneath our shop in Islington, London. This recipe adaptation will let you brew your own all grain version of our 'Citra Pale ale;' we have also developed 1.3 gallon (5L) 'brew in a bag' homebrew kits for beginners.

Recipe: Brewer in Residence, Daniel Price

BASICS

VOLUME	5 gallons (20L)
BOIL VOLUME	6.6 gallons (25L)
ABV	4.3–4.8%
TARGET FG	1010–1021
TARGET OG	1047
PH	5.5

METHOD AND TIMINGS

MASH	
Temperature	**Time**
154°F (68°C)	60 min.

FERMENTATION
64°F (18°C)

INGREDIENTS

MALT	
Pale	7lb (3.2kg)
Munich	8oz (0.227kg)
Amber	8oz (0.227kg)

HOPS			
	Weight	Addition time	Attribute
Northern Brewer	0.49oz (14g)	60 min.	Bittering
Citra	0.25oz (7g)	30 min.	Aroma
Citra	0.49oz (14g)	0 min.	Aroma
Citra	0.35oz (10g)	Dry hop	

YEAST
WLP001

BREWERS' TIP
To get great clarity in your pale beers it is important to cool your wort efficiently before pitching for a quick cold break. Chilling the beer after fermentation and a dry hop is also important: this is called a 'cold crash' and helps any particles drop out of the beer.

IPA

PUNK IPA

BREWDOG
5.6% ABV

Brewdog is responsible for a great deal of the momentum behind craft beer in the UK (and beyond). It recently published recipes for every single beer it has ever brewed through its *DIY Dog* initiative, including 'Punk IPA.' This is the brewery's flagship beer, and a great example of a modern interpretation of a classic style. Don't stop with this recipe though – visit www.brewdog.com/lowdown/diydog and try them all!

Recipe: Brewdog DIY Dog

BASICS

VOLUME	5 gallons (20L)
BOIL VOLUME	6.6 gallons (25L)
ABV	5.6%
TARGET FG	1011
TARGET OG	1053
PH	4.4

METHOD AND TIMINGS

MASH	
Temperature	Time
152°F (66°C)	75 min.

FERMENTATION
66°F (19°C)

BREWERS' TIP
To get the best possible profile from the dry hops it is recommended that you dry hop post fermentation for five days. Dry hops should be added at cellar temperature; 57.2°F (14°C) which results in the most aromatic dry hop profile.

INGREDIENTS

MALT

Extra pale	9.6lb (4.38kg)
Caramalt	8.82oz (0.25kg)

HOPS

	Weight	Addition time	Attribute
Chinook	0.7oz (20g)	60 min.	Bitter
Ahtanum	0.44oz (12.5g)	60 min.	Bitter
Chinook	0.7oz (20g)	30 min.	Flavour
Ahtanum	0.44oz (12.5g)	30 min.	Flavour
Chinook	0.97oz (27.5g)	0 min.	Flavour
Ahtanum	0.44oz (12.5g)	0 min.	Flavour
Simcoe	0.44oz (12.5g)	0 min.	Flavour

HOPS

	Weight	Addition time	Attribute
Nelson Sauvin	0.44oz (12.5g)	0 min.	Flavour
Chinook	1.68oz (47.5g)	Dry hop	
Ahtanum	1.32oz (37.5g)	Dry hop	
Simcoe	1.32oz (37.5g)	Dry hop	
Nelson Sauvin	0.7oz (20g)	Dry hop	
Cascade	1.32oz (37.5g)	Dry hop	
Amarillo	0.35oz (10g)	Dry hop	

YEAST

Wyeast 1056 – American Ale™

RED ALE

SOMETHING BREWED

ADNAMS
4.5% ABV

When I got married in 2014, Adnams kindly agreed to let me brew a beer for my wedding on their pilot kit. I went for a red ale (my favourite style), with bags of New World hops – Mosaic (for Mitch) and Simcoe (for Sarah, my wife). Belinda Jennings came up with the original recipe and brewed with me, and I cannot thank her and head brewer Fergus Fitzgerald enough for helping me have a beautiful beer at my wedding!

BASICS

VOLUME	5 gallons (20L)
BOIL VOLUME	6.6 gallons (25L)
ABV	4.5%
TARGET FG	1011
TARGET OG	1045
PH	5.2

METHOD AND TIMINGS

MASH	
Temperature	Time
155°F (68°C)	60 min.

FERMENTATION
64°F (18°C)

INGREDIENTS

MALT	
Pale ale malt	7.5lb (3.4kg)
Munich II	14.1oz (400g)
Rye malt	12.34oz (350g)
Amber malt	6.35oz (180g)
Crystal 90	4.94oz (140g)
Chocolate	1.76oz (50g)

HOPS			
	Weight	Addition time	Attribute
Chinook	0.7oz (20g)	60 min.	Bitter
Simcoe	0.28oz (8g)	45 min.	Bitter
Mosaic	0.67oz (19g)	10 min.	Aroma
Mosaic	1.06oz (30g)	0 min.	Aroma

BREWERS' TIP

Adnams beers are typically quite sulfurous, which is reminiscent of being by the sea. The sulfur notes are a combination of the yeasts and the mineral content of the water. Use a Burton yeast if you can't get hold of Adnams' house strain.

YEAST
Adnams House Yeast

PORTER

EXPORT INDIA PORTER

THE KERNEL
6.0% ABV

Evin O'Riordain started The Kernel in
Bermondsey, London, after visiting New
York in 2007 and having a beer epiphany.
The initial inspiration for this recipe came
from a Durden Park Beer Circle pamphlet
entitled *Old British Beers and How To
Make Them*. This may not be quite the old
Barclay Perkins or Whitbread beer it was
based on, but the ingredients available
have changed, as have people's palates.
As Evin says: "We want to make a beer
that we want to drink, rather than make
a beer that we think servicemen in India
in the 19th century would have wanted to
drink. So, changes are inevitable."

BASICS

VOLUME	5 gallons (20L)
BOIL VOLUME	6.6 gallons (25L)
ABV	6.0%
TARGET FG	1016
TARGET OG	1060
PH	6
IBU	45–48

METHOD AND TIMINGS

MASH	
Temperature	Time
153°F (67°C)	60 min.

FERMENTATION
68°F (20°C)

INGREDIENTS

MALT	
Marris Otter pale	9.04lb (4.1kg)
Brown malt	14.46oz (410g)
Chocolate	14.46oz (410g)
Crystal	14.46oz (410g)
Black	7.05oz (200g)

HOPS			
	Weight	Addition time	Attribute
Bramling X (6%)	1.05oz (30g)	First wort hop*	Bitterness
Bramling X (6%)	1.05oz (30g)	15 min.	Flavour
Bramling X (6%)	1.05oz (30g)	15 min.	Flavour
Bramling X (6%)	2.10oz (60g)	5 min.	Flavour
Bramling X (6%)	2.82oz (80g)	Dry hop	Aroma

BREWERS' TIP

Use 0.12oz (3.5g) of priming sugar per ¼ gallon (1 litre) and condition for 10–12 days to produce approximately 2.4 volumes of CO_2.

First wort hopping is when bittering hops are added before the wort is brought to the boil.

YEAST
House ale yeast (or a London strain)

GROW

So you've got the basics down, you're happy brewing and you're enjoying the beers you've made. What next? Well, despite having just four key ingredients, a small variation in each – or any of the control points during the brew – can have a significant impact on your beer. Ultimately, this means there is a near-infinite array of different beers just waiting to be brewed by you.

But how do you know how to narrow it down? How can you make sure your precious time spent on brew days isn't in vain? This chapter aims to help you get a better understanding of how you can play with recipes, techniques and styles to achieve some great results. We couldn't possibly cover everything, but we can definitely point you in the right direction so you can grow and develop your brewing abilities.

GO ONLINE

Before you try to evolve your brewing I highly recommend you brew some staples regularly. Mastering and maintaining consistency on simpler brews will hone your skills so that you have more control when you decide to brew something more adventurous.

SOCIAL BREWING

When you are ready to expand your recipe portfolio you'll want to make sure you have some good resources, and there are plenty of brilliant homebrew forums online and on social media. No matter far out your idea is, there is a fair chance that somebody in the global homebrew community has had a go before, and they'll most likely be happy to share their observations and top tips with you. Here are a few recommended resources to explore:

Facebook Groups
UK Homebrewing Community
Homebrew Network

Forums
www.thehomebrewforum.co.uk
forum.craftbrewing.org.uk
www.jimsbeerkit.co.uk/forum/

ADAPTING OR 'PIMPING' EXTRACT RECIPES

The recipes in the previous chapter are all grain recipes, but brewing with kits or extract can be a lot more time efficient. The initial outlay is also much lower. However, that doesn't mean you can't experiment, and there are several ways you can 'pimp' any extract kit:

VARYING THE HOPS

The hops for the original recipes are usually included, but you can vary the hop amounts or include different hops for a twist. Trying the same recipe with different single hop batches is a great way of learning what flavours certain hops impart.

DRY HOPPING

Most kits are fairly simple, and dry hopping isn't usually part of the process. However, there's nothing stopping you from getting your hands on some more hops and adding a 3–5 day dry hop post fermentation for a bigger aroma.

ADDING EXTRACT

You can buy different malt extracts, so why not give them a go? For example, you could try replacing some of the pre-made kit extract in an IPA with some black malt extract to create a black IPA.

To help you calculate changes to your recipes you can use home-brewing software such as BeerSmith (www.beersmith.com)

DESIGNING YOUR OWN RECIPES

As well as helping you out when you want to 'pimp' a recipe, home-brewing software such as BeerSmith will also prove invaluable if, or when, you decide to design your own recipes. This can simply be a result of wanting to create something unique, or because changes might be necessary due to the availability of ingredients.

KEEPING TRACK

If you are setting out to create your own brew it is also vital that you have a solid amount of information on your past brews. The efficiency of your brewkit and the pH of the water you use will all have a bearing on how your brew turns out.

ADAPTING

My advice is to start by adapting recipes that are tried and tested. Switch one or two ingredients out for different ones, such as using darker malts in a pale ale recipe for a red ale, or substituting some roasted and chocolate malts to an IPA for a black IPA.

LAGER

BROOKLYN LAGER

BROOKLYN BREWERY
5.2% ABV

Lagers are notoriously difficult to brew, not just due to the requirements for efficient and accurate cooling. Small errors in hygiene or process will cause 'off flavours' from malt, yeast or water and with low bitterness from delicate hop additions there is nowhere to hide. Garrett Oliver, once a homebrewer himself, provided us with the recipe for this iconic brew. A Vienna-style lager, with slightly darker malts, a rich full body and a citrussy, orangey finish. It's no wonder this is the brewery's flagship beer.

Recipe: Brooklyn Brewery Brewmaster, Garrett Oliver

BASICS

VOLUME	5 gallons (20L)
BOIL VOLUME	6.6 gallons (25L)
ABV	5.2%
TARGET FG	1012
TARGET OG	1048
PH	5.4

METHOD AND TIMINGS

MASH	
Temperature	**Time**
116°F (47°C)	20 min.
135°F (57°C)	5 min.
156°F (69°C)	35 min.

FERMENTATION
55°F (13°C) until fermentation starts.
Reduce to 52°F(11°C) for the remainder.
Rise to 61°F (16°C) for 48 hrs post fermentation.
Reduce to 36°F (2.2°C) for lagering (17 days).

INGREDIENTS

HOPS			
	Weight	Addition time	Attribute
Willamette	0.99oz (28g)	75 min.	Bittering
Cascade	0.33oz (9.25g)	35 min.	Bittering
Vanguard	0.44oz (12.6g)	35 min.	Bittering
Hallertau Mittelfruh	0.49oz (14g)	2 min.	Aroma
Saphir	0.49oz (14g)	2 min.	Aroma
Cascade	0.49oz (14g)	2 min.	Aroma
Hallertau Mittelfruh	1.48oz (42g)	7 days	Dry hop
Cascade	0.74oz (21g)	7 days	Dry hop

MALT	
American 2-row	9.6lb (4.25kg)
Munich (10 'L)	14oz (0.4kg)
Caramel malt (60'L)	11oz (0.3kg)

BREWERS' TIP

To reach the saccharification temperature of 156 °F (69 °C), there are two methods, depending on your equipment. If your heat source can raise the temperature of the mash rapidly (5–10 mins), then do so. If not, add very hot water at 200 °F (93 °C) to the mash, stirring vigorously to avoid hot spots, until you reach the target temperature. The reason for this procedure is that American 2-row malt is diastatically powerful, and if the mash isn't heated quickly enough, the resulting wort will be too fermentable.

YEAST
White Labs 833 (German bock lager)

STEAM BEER

CANONBURY COMMON

BREWERY BELOW
4.6% ABV

Pale lagers like hells and pilsner styles
have a very delicate malt character
and are very lightly hopped. This light
delicate flavour means that any brewing
mistakes or even mild infections are
easily discernible. There is nowhere
to hide, the skill of the brewer is on full
show. When Europeans first moved to
the United States and started to brew
traditional styles, they didn't have access
to the natural cooling they had been
used to in Northern Europe and steam
beers were born. Generally a darker,
or Vienna style lager, these are more
straightforward to brew at home.

Recipe: Brewer in Residence, Daniel Price

BASICS

VOLUME	5 gallons (20L)
BOIL VOLUME	6.6 gallons (25L)
ABV	4.6%
TARGET FG	1012
TARGET OG	1048
PH	5.4

METHOD AND TIMINGS

MASH	
Temperature	Time
155°F (68°C)	60 min.

FERMENTATION
64°F (18°C)

INGREDIENTS

MALT	
Pale	6.6lb (3kg)
Munich	17.6oz (0.5kg)
Carapils	17.6oz (0.5kg)
Crystal 40	3.5oz (0.1kg)

HOPS			
	Weight	Addition time	Attribute
Northern Brewer	0.70oz (20g)	start	Bittering
Northern Brewer	0.42oz (12g)	0 min.	Aroma
Cascade	0.70oz (20g)	-	Dry hop

YEAST
WhiteLabs WLP0810

BREWERS' TIP

Once fermentation has finished, leave the beer to 'rest' for an extra couple of days. This extra time at fermentation temperature is called 'diacetyl rest' and will reduce the risk of buttery off flavours.

SOUR BEERS

Sour beers are so called because of their tart, sharp and often acidic flavour. Much like the first beers brewed, this is due to the impact of wild yeast or bacteria on the beer. Since Louis Pasteur taught us about controlling yeast and improvements in hygiene standards, most beers no longer have this characterisitic. It has been mainly the Belgians who kept these flavours alive through lambic beers, gueuze and Flemish red ales. Now coming back into vogue, there are several methods commonly used to brew sour ales.

LACTOBACILLUS

It is also possible to sour a beer in the fermenter by adding *Lactobacillus* bacteria after the beer has been brewed. This is by the far the quickest method, but often considered the least authentic.

CAUTION

If any yeast and bacteria manage to survive in a nook or crevice you didn't clean properly you could spoil future beers. Therefore, moving sour or infected beer around a brewery isn't a great idea if you intend to produce 'normal' beers with the same equipment.

KETTLE SOUR

Kettle sours are produced using a normal wort that is boiled to get rid of any unpredictable bacteria. A live culture is then added (yogurt works well) or a small amount of grain in a bag to mimic a sour mash. If the wort is then kept warm (around 113°F / 45°C) for a few days, the pH should start to drop. It's important to check regularly, and once the pH drops to your desired level (around 3.5–4.5 for a *Berliner Weisse*) you should boil the wort and then transfer it.

SOUR MASH

Sour mash is created when the mash tun – containing grain and water – is left warm for several days. Wild yeasts in the grain start to ferment and sour the wort. Once it has reached the desired 'sourness' the mash is sparged with additional water, moved to the kettle and boiled to kill any now-unwanted bacteria.

LAMBIC & WILD BEERS

Lambic beers are soured using natural wild yeasts from the surrounding environment. This type of beer uses open fermentation, which means it is not something that is easily replicated, although the Belgians have been passing this skill down from brewer to brewer for many years.

However, there are some wild yeasts that have been semi-cultivated, such as *Brettanomyces*, or 'Brett.' In the wild, Brett lives on the skins of fruit and in both beer and wine making contamination is usually considered a fault. However, in some beers and wines, its 'barnyard' or 'horse-blanket' character is desirable. Brett also works well alongside other yeasts: the Belgian beer, Orval, is inoculated with Brett in the bottle and is a wonderful example of its charm.

CAUTION

Intentionally inoculating your beer with *Brettanomyces* alongside your original yeast can result in some wonderfully complex flavours, but you need to be careful. Brett is an aggressive yeast that leaves very little sugar (bone dry beers) and lots of fizz: you will have to use strong bottles if you don't want your beer store to be destroyed by bottle bombs!

FLAVOURING BEER

Beers can develop wonderful flavours from just the four key elements, but outside of the German purity law there is nothing to say that beer can't include other ingredients.

ADDING FLAVOUR
Ingredients can be added during the mash, to the boil or in the fermenter. I would recommend post-fermentation flavouring, which can bring some beautiful results.

FERMENTATION
Adding your ingredients to the fermenter at low temperatures gives a beautiful freshness that captures fruit and other flavours perfectly. Before you add anything, you need to make sure it is clean. A quick dip in a pan of very hot water will work for most whole fruit, herbs, spices or coffee beans, ensuring you don't spoil your beer before you get to try it.

COFFEE IPA   PEANUT BUTTER STOUT   RASPBERRY WHEAT   SOUR FRUIT BERLINER WEISSE

COFFEE STOUT

THERE ARE MANY FLAVOURED BEER STYLES THAT HAVE BEEN DONE
BEFORE, SO THERE WILL BE PLENTY OF HELP ONLINE.
SOME OF THE OPTIONS INCLUDE:

BLOOD ORANGE IPA   PINK GRAPEFRUIT SESSION IPA   CHILLI PORTER   THAI BASIL SAISON

SOUR BEER

TART PASSIONFRUIT RASPBERRY WIT

SOUL REBEL BREW CO.
5.25% ABV

'Gypsy brewers' travel from brewery to brewery making their beer using different kit with different people, renting brewhouses or collaborating on recipes with accommodating brewmasters. Dan Price is just such a person: he was Head Brewer at Weird Beard Brewing Co. and London Brewing Co. and has collaborated with Brodies, Mad Hatter, Elusive, Summer Wine, Outlaw, Hanging Bat and now The Brewery Below. Dan's free-spirited approach to beer has also led to some 'alternative' brewing practices that appear under the Soul Rebel Brew Co. banner.

Recipe: Daniel Price

BASICS

VOLUME	5 gallons (20L)
BOIL VOLUME	6.6 gallons (25L)
ABV	5.25%
TARGET FG	1008
TARGET OG	1048
PH	5.2–5.5

METHOD AND TIMINGS

MASH	
Temperature	Time
154°F (68°C)	60 min.

FERMENTATION
64°F (18°C)

INGREDIENTS

MALT

MALT	
Pale	3.53lb (1.6kg)
Wheat	4.41lb (2kg)
Munich	7.94oz (225g)
Rice hulls	7.94oz (225g)

HOPS

	Weight	Addition time	Attribute
Northern Brewer	0.49oz (14g)	60 min.	Bittering

YEAST

YEAST
WLP410

FRUIT

	Weight
Passion fruit puree	16.74 US fl oz (475ml)
Raspberry puree	32.12 US fl oz (950ml

Once fermented, remove from yeast, add the fruit purees and age for two weeks, shaking occasionally. Settle cold and remove the beer from the settled sediment. Carbonate and serve.

BREWERS' TIP
You can sour this beer in a Berliner Weisse style by adding yoghurt culture to the wort. Leave it for a few days at 118°F (48°C), until the pH drops to around 3.5–4, and then continue with the boil and fermentation.

AGEING BEER IN BARRELS

Historically, beer and wood have had a long relationship and it is only with relatively recent advancements in technology that we have moved to steel (or plastic) vessels for fermenting and conditioning beer.

WHICH BARREL TO CHOOSE?

The first challenge for a homebrewer is to find a barrel to use. An old spirit barrel works well, but think about flavours that match: dark beers work well with dark spirits or red wine, while lighter beers are better suited to light spirits or white wine. Burgundy, Sauternes and bourbon barrels are the most sought after by brewers.

FILLING THE BARREL

Once you have a barrel, the next challenge is to fill it! If you don't fill it completely, the beer will oxidize too much and too quickly. A great way for homebrewers to barrel age beer is to club together, brew the same beer and add all of the batches to the barrel.

SANITIZING

If you don't want to risk souring your beer, it is wise to sanitize your barrel before you begin. Steam is ideal for this, but a good slosh with boiling water will also work. If there is alcohol left in the barrel from its previous use this will also help kill any unwanted bacteria, as well as adding a layer of complexity to a finished beer.

TIME

Beers with a high alcohol content have more resistance to bacteria and spoilage by wild yeast, but you should avoid opening the barrel regularly: seal it, leave it and have faith. Three to six months is a good time to leave a dark barrel-aged beer, while a pale saison aged in a Sauternes barrel might need less time in the wood.

BARREL-AGED BEER

BARREL-AGED IMPERIAL STOUT

BOSS
11% ABV

Chris is a very good friend of mine, who
I got to know when I ran The Thatchers
Arms on the borders of Essex and Suffolk
in the UK. Chris has now moved back to
the USA and is part of a homebrew group
known as the 'Brewers of Siloam Springs'
(BOSS). In 2015 the group clubbed
together and each brewed a batch of
this beer, which they then added to a
Four Roses Bourbon barrel. I was lucky
enough to share a bottle with him when
I visited him in Arkansas in 2015. It was
absolutely stunning!

Recipe: Chris Butler

BASICS

VOLUME	5 gallons (20L)
BOIL VOLUME	6.6 gallons (25L)
ABV	11%
TARGET FG	1008
TARGET OG	1020
PH	6

METHOD AND TIMINGS

MASH	
Temperature	Time
155°F (68°C)	60 min.

FERMENTATION
64°F (18°C)

INGREDIENTS

MALT	
Maris Otter	3.09lb (1.4kg)
Pale Maris Otter	10.56lb (4.79kg)
Chocolate malt	1.65lb (740g)
Roasted barley	1.54lb (700g)
Caramunich	12oz (340g)
Caravienne	12oz (340g)
Candi sugar	14.1oz (400g)

YEAST
London Ale Yeast (wyeast 1028)

HOPS			
	Weight	Addition time	Attribute
Northern Brewer	1.5oz (42g)	45 min.	Bittering
Northern Brewer	1oz (28g)	30 min.	Mixed
Northern Brewer	12oz (340g)	0 min.	Aroma

BREWERS' TIP

BOSS used two packs of yeast for this beast to get it to the high target ABV. The Candi sugar also helps and is best added just after the boil has started, about 10 minutes into the process. The beer was left in the barrel for around four months, allowing it to pick up plenty of barrel and bourbon flavours.

HOMEBREW CLUBS & COMPETITIONS

It might be enough for some homebrewers to just enjoy their own beers, but for those looking to see what other people are brewing and how their efforts shape up against them, homebrew competitions are extremely popular. Many homebrew clubs have their own competitions and some breweries also host them – the prize is often for the winning beer to be brewed commercially.

IN THE UNITED KINGDOM

The supermarket chain Waitrose – along with The Thornbridge Brewery and BrewUK – has supported The Great British Homebrew Challenge since 2014, while The UK National Homebrew Competition is one of the biggest competitions in Great Britain.

IN THE UNITED STATES

The American Homebrewers Association has a host of information on competitions around the country. It also runs the world's largest international beer competition – the 'National Homebrew Competition' (NHC). Entries for this prestigious event are usually taken in February via the Association's website, www.homebrewersassociation.org.

HOMEBREW CLUBS

Homebrew clubs are popping up all over the world. Sharing ideas with other brewers is a great way to learn, and joining a club will give you the opportunity to swap recipes, discuss techniques and equipment, and get honest feedback from other brewers on the beers you're producing.

HOMEBREW CLUBS

The best way to find a group near to you is to search online or ask at your local homebrew supplies shop or brewery. Many commercial brewers started out as homebrewers and still brew at home to try out new recipes or ones they want to drink, but might struggle to sell!

TURNING IT INTO A BUSINESS

So you're brewing like a pro, you've won a heap of competitions and your friends all want your beer. Maybe it's time to take a leap of faith and turn your passion and hobby into a business, but what do you need to know from a business point of view?

LEGALITY

In the UK, even though it is legal to brew without a license, it is illegal to sell any alcohol without being registered with HMRC and paying duty, not even to friends and family. It is legal for other people to contribute to the cost of ingredients, so you don't always have to be out of pocket.

REGISTRATION

Registration for a brewing license in the UK is simple, but can take up to six weeks. Once registered you will have to complete regular duty returns for HMRC who will charge you duty for the alcohol you've produced, based on the 'duty returns' they require from you. You will also need to register for AWRS (Alcohol Wholesale Registration Scheme).

IN THE UNITED STATES

In the United States, adults may produce up to 100 gallons of beer per year for personal consumption without a license or paying taxes. Brew more than that and you'll need to apply for approval from the Alcohol and Tobacco Tax and Trade Bureau. If you want to sell your beer you'll need a state wholesaler's license.

ONSITE CONSUMPTION

In both countries you'll need another whole level of paperwork if you want to sell beer to be consumed onsite, or direct to the public in a shop, bar or taproom.

REMEMBER

Licenses and practices in different countries vary greatly and, although these are a rough guide, please make sure you have checked your local laws before you persue any new venture.

BUSINESS PLAN

After you've sorted out the legalities of your brewing venture, the next step is drawing up a business plan. Even if you aren't asking for a loan or investment, it is great practice to have a clear idea about the road ahead. A business plan can always be changed if needed, but having that vision written down might just keep you headed in the right direction.

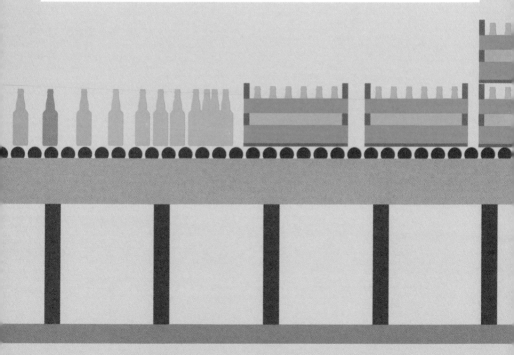

INVESTMENT

The most obvious thing about scaling up your business is that you need to produce more of your brew, and to do this you need to increase your brewing capacity. Brewery kits and installation can be found through quality suppliers ranging from £10,000 ($12,500) upwards.

EQUIPMENT

Invest in your fermenters, they limit your production quality and quantity far more than anything else. Well-insulated vessels with good temperature control can be expensive, but they'll be worth it in the long run.

SPACE ISN'T EVERYTHING

Seren Brewery in Carmarthenshire is a commercial brewery that was housed in a 9ft ($2.7m^2$) square room in brewer Ali's house. Remember, though, it's not just the brewkit and fermenters you need space for, there are kegs, casks, bottles, cleaning materials and scope for expansion that all need to be considered!

BRANDING

Invest in your branding, good beer will get people coming back, but you need to get them to make the first purchase! See www.beermarketingawards.co.uk for some great examples, and www.pumpclipparade.co.uk for the worst the industry has to offer!

THE CUSTOMER IS ALWAYS RIGHT

Finally, listen to what your customers want; they're buying it, not you!

VIEW FROM THE BREWER: OLI WATTS

WATTS BREW CO., SUFFOLK
HOMEBREWER WHO TURNED SEMI-PRO IN 2015

Q You started out on a 1 barrel kit, is this your only source of income?

A No. It's a weekend and evening side project at the moment.

Q Your brewery is at home in your garage, did you require any other planning or licenses?

A I contacted the local council and asked what permission I required. Planning wasn't needed because I'm only doing it part time. I also required trade waste permission. Like the council, the water company were very helpful. They visited to offer advice and took what I was trying to do seriously.

Q What advice would you give to somebody else starting out as you did?

A Don't be afraid of asking advice. Twitter has been incredibly useful and I have had some great advice from pro brewers – most of whom I've not even met.

Don't skimp on the kit. I invested in the biggest I could afford. I could have DIY'd it, but having something purpose-made helps consistency. Invest in getting your drainage and floor right. I installed a channel drain in the garage. It was an annoyance, but I couldn't live without it.

Finally, savour the first moment you see someone drinking your beer in a pub. It's an amazing feeling.

VIEW FROM THE BREWER: MARK TRANTER

BURNING SKY, EAST SUSSEX
HOMEBREWER AND PROFESSIONAL BREWER OF OVER 20 YEARS

Q It's been three years since you set up Burning Sky, what's the most important piece of kit any professional brewer should invest in?

A Yourself, followed by everything else. Spend as much as you can on the various items that comprise a brewery – if you are looking to expand at some point, then purchase ancillary items such as chilling plants that are 'future proof.'

Q There are a handful of commercial nanobreweries out there making it work (Watts and Seren *et al*), in your opinion what size brewlength is a sensible viable commercial option?

A That all depends on your own aspirations and experience. Less than 5bbl's is going to be a struggle to be commercially viable in my opinion – you don't spend five times the amount of money doing a 5bbl brewery as opposed to a 1bbl brewery. To upgrade is expensive, time consuming and incredibly disruptive to production and your mental well being.

Q You've been brewing commercially for over 20 years, but what would you advise is the biggest leap for somebody coming from a homebrewing background?

A Dealing with HMRC, sourcing raw ingredient suppliers and having a scary amount of beer to sell!

Q What's your final piece of advice for any budding brewery start-ups?

A Try not to follow trends – be true to yourself and make the beers that you want to drink to the very best of your ability. If you believe in what you are doing, people will follow you.

GLOSSARY

alcohol by volume (ABV)
The measurement of the percentage of alcohol in a volume of beer.

ale
A top-fermenting beer brewed at warmer temperatures between 59–68 °F (15–20 °C).

alpha acid
A chemical compound found in the resin gland of the hop plant. It is the source of bitterness in hops.

Dimethyl sulfide (DMS)
A sulfur compound produced during fermentation of beer. It generally has a disagreeable flavour.

dry hopping
The addition of hops post boil to produce an intense bitterness.

fermentation
The conversion of sugar, by yeast, into alcohol and CO_2.

hydrometer
An instrument used to measure the specific gravity of a liquid.

International Bittering Units (IBU)
Universal measurement of bitterness in beer.

lager
A bottom-fermenting beer produced at low temperatures, that matures during cold storage.

lambic
A type of beer, typically produced in a small area of Belgium, that is fermented naturally by wild yeasts.

mash
The process of steeping malt in water to extract to extract fermentable sugars.

pH scale
A scale, from 0 to 14, to measure the acidity (0) or alkalinity (14) of a solution.

sparge
Sparging, also known as lautering, is a process where hot water is poured over the grain bed to rinse out any sugars.

wort
The wort is the liquid product of the mashing process and is the extract of the malt that contains the sugars.

RESOURCES

BOOKS

The Oxford Companion to Beer,
Garrett Oliver, Oxford University
Press, 2011

How to Brew, John Palmer,
Brewers Publications, 2006

Hops & Glory, Pete Brown,
Pan MacMillan, 2010

WEB SITES

www.howtobrew.com
An invaluable resource for
homebrewers

www.worldbeerawards.com
World beer awards

www.bjcp.org
Beer judge certification program

BREWERIES

Adnams Brewery
Sole Bay Brewery, Southwold, Suffolk,
IP18 6JW, England
www.adnams.co.uk

BrewDog
Balmacassie Industrial Estate, Ellon,
Aberdeenshire, AB41 8BX, Scotland
www.brewdog.com

The Brewery Below
Borough Wines & Beers, 344A Essex
Road, London, N1 3PD, England

Brooklyn Brewery
79 N 11th St. Brooklyn, NY 11249,
United States,
www.brooklynbrewery.com

Burning Sky Brewery
Place Barn, The Street, Firle,
East Sussex, BN8 6LP, England
www.burningskybeer.com

The Kernel Brewery
Arch 11, Dockley Road Industrial
Estate, London, SE16 3SF, England
www.thekernelbrewery.com

London Brewing Co
762 High Road, North Finchley,
London, N12 9QH, England
www.londonbrewing.com

Watts Brew Co.
www.watts.fm

INDEX

ACKNOWLEDGMENTS

This book is dedicated to my wife Sarah, a very understanding beer widow, no more so than whilst I was writing this book. I would like to thank her, and the rest of my family, for all of the support and encouragement I received.

As well as the brewers who gave their time for interviews or to include recipes, I would especially like to thank a couple of friends in the brewing industry for their help, knowledge and advice, Pete Brown, Adrian Tierney-Jones, Daniel Price from The Brewery Below and Dan Fox from London Brewing Co..

Finally a huge thank you to Jason Hook, Jamie Pumfrey and the team at Ammonite Press for their unwavering support and guidance.

AMMONITE
PRESS

www.ammonitepress.com